# Where Do I Live?

by

## SHIRLEY GREENWAY

photographs by

## OXFORD SCIENTIFIC FILMS

Ideals Children's Books     Nashville, Tennessee

Published by Ideals Publishing Corporation
Nashville, Tennessee 37214

Printed and bound in Mexico.

Created and designed by Treld Bicknell.

**Library of Congress Cataloging-in-Publication Data**

Greenway, Shirley.
Where do I live?/by Shirley Greenway; photographs by
Oxford Scientific Films.
p.  cm.
Summary: Depicts animals in their natural habitats and
explains how they live and interact with their
environment.
ISBN 0-8249-8576-1 (lib. bdg.)
ISBN 0-8249-8561-3 (trade pbk.)
1. Animals—Habitations—Juvenile literature.  [1.
Animals—Habitat.]  I. Oxford Scientific Films.  II. Title.
QL756.G64   1992
599'.056'4—dc20                                    92-7739
                                                              CIP
                                                              AC

Acknowledgments:
The author and publisher wish to thank the following for permission to reproduce copyrighted material: **Oxford
Scientific Films** for front cover and p. 17 (Laurence Gould); p. 2 (Animals Animals–Henry Ausloos); back cover, pp. 4
and 5 (Edwin Sadd); p. 6 (AA–Breck P. Kent); p. 7 (G.I. Bernard); title page and p. 22 (Okapi-Hans Reinhard); pp. 8,
10-11 (Michael Fogden); p. 12 (James H. Robinson); pp. 13 and 15 (Lon E. Lauber); p. 14 (Tom Ulrich); p. 16 (Max
Gibbs); pp. 18, 20-21 (Ben Osborne); p. 23 (AA–Ted Levin); p. 24 (AA-Margot Conte); p. 25 (AA–John Gerlach); pp. 26
and 27 (David MacDonald); p. 28 (Richard Kolar); and p. 29 (Frank Huber).

I am a wolf.

Where do I live?

A. Wolves live in families, or packs, among the tall trees of northern forests. They hunt together during the day and shelter out of sight in the cold, night hours.

**Q.** I am an elephant.

Where do I live?

**A.** Led by the oldest female, African elephants live in herds in the African bush. They are the largest of all the land-dwelling animals.

I am a fox.

Where do I live?

 The cunning red fox lives in a den which the vixen digs under a woody bank. Her home is called an earth, where her cubs are safely hidden.

**Q.** I am a snake.

Where do I live?

**A.** The eyelash viper lives in the rainforests of Central America. It is small, beautiful, and deadly. Its bright yellow body stands out clearly against the rich jungle colors, luring prey and warning predators.

I am a goat.

Where do I live?

 The nimble mountain goat makes its home on the craggiest peaks of the Rocky Mountains. It is the perfect place for the world's most sure-footed animal mountaineer.

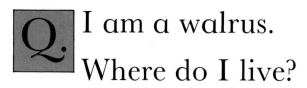 I am a walrus.
Where do I live?

A. The wrinkly, long-tusked walrus is a very sociable animal. When not hunting for food on the seabed, walruses like to gather on a rocky beach to snooze in the sun with several close friends.

**Q.** I am a goldfish.
Where do I live?

**A.** This goldfish has a very large bowl to swim in—the brilliant waters of the Red Sea. Sea goldfish are also called jewelfish, and it is easy to see why as they swim in glittering shoals among the many-colored shapes of the coral reefs.

Q. I am a seal.

Where do I live?

**A.** Seals love water and rocky beaches. Some seals prefer the cold water and floating ice of the Arctic Ocean; others like the sunny shores of warmer seas. But to find the deep-diving Weddell (WED · el) seal, you must go south to the coldest place on earth—Antarctica. The solitary Weddells spend most of their time fishing in icy waters and stop to rest on an ice floe.

**Q.** I am a beaver.
Where do I live?

**A.** Beavers are clever builders. They cut down trees with their big front teeth to dam rivers and streams. Here, in a roomy lodge built of twigs, bark, and river mud, beavers spend the snowy winters, safe and warm.

I am a squirrel.

Where do I live?

 The agile, bushy-tailed squirrel is
perfectly at home in a tall tree—
scampering along its branches and up
and down the trunk with ease. Squirrels
make a cozy nest in the fork of a leafy
branch or in a hollow trunk.

I am a meerkat.
Where do I live?

A. A slender meerkat stands at attention on a rocky mound. He is on lookout duty, protecting the entrance to the underground burrow where the young meerkats are tended by an adult. Meerkats work very hard to survive in their African desert home.

I am an alligator.
Where do I live?

 The scaly, broad-nosed American alligator spends its life swimming and feeding in the warm fresh waters of southern swampland rivers and lazing on sunny riverbanks.

# Animals live in many different places:

The wolf lives in the forest.

The eyelash viper lives i the rainfore

The elephant lives in the bush.

The goat lives on the mountain.

The fox lives in an under-ground den.

The walrus lives on a rocky shore

 The goldfish lives in the sea.

 The squirrel lives in a tree.

 The seal lives on the ice.

 The meerkat lives in a desert burrow.

 The beaver lives in a lodge.

 The alligator lives on a riverbank.

# Index